Unstoppable Utopia

Unstoppable Utopia

Cassandra Moss

Wild Honey Press

Copyright © Cassandra Moss, 2025

ISBN 978-1-903090-63-3

Typesetting by Margaret Healy

Wild Honey Press
16a Ballyman Road
Enniskerry
County Wicklow
A98 KX99
Ireland

www.wildhoneypress.com

The self wants in its despair to savour to the full the satisfaction of making itself into itself, of developing itself; it wants to take the credit for this fictional, masterly project, its own way of understanding itself. And yet what it understands itself to be is in the final instance a riddle; just when it seems on the point of having the building finished, at a whim it can dissolve the whole thing into nothing.
                    -Søren Kierkegaard, *The Sickness Unto Death*

CONTENTS

Work

Work Away	11
Work Around	14
Work Out	20
Work On	26
Work Up	28
Work Through	31

Life

Plastics	52
In the time when no vessels were flights	53
Plague Times	54
A person of	57
St. Margery Without	59
windows might	60

WORK

WORK AWAY

My parents are blunt instruments
says Jane the co-worker with her redwine mouth
like concrete slabs
on a very wet day
swinging at head height

The cooling mid-October air inhales her expelled cigarette smoke
to breathe it out all over again onto your listening face

You think of the last time you spoke to your father
as you and your colleagues are decanted
from one pub to another
and conclude
it's you who's the sharp one

Throughout the night you get prickles
of a sense that everything will still be alright in time

In between them
you look over at Jane
to see her particular kind of devastation
hanging like a second lanyard
around her neck

When the time comes
you put your round on credit card
to avoid dipping
into your overdraft

Jane has just moved on from Paula to John

You think of how John's malice
is locked into his eyes
making office exchanges with him
the sort of task you put off
until the need is dire
until you have to look him in the eye
and bolt your skeleton to your skin
to keep it from escaping

In 1998 you watched a TV show
where people taught at a school and went drinking together
and you surmised their lives
were the result of specific choices
fetching coordinated outcomes

You enter in the middle
of Rob going on at Sophie

about that new thing on the telly
in which someone good does something bad

and he's saying how he waited
to watch
one episode after the other
in an unbroken stream

and in his tone
you feel his compulsion
you feel his fervour
to remove himself
from himself
to suspend his own passing
on fictional hooks

In 1998 your time was clearly segmented
into one episode per week
which peculiarly made you feel even more smothered
by the drama of others

Yet they were simpler times back then
weren't they?

WORK AROUND

"No, I actually like to laugh. I like receiving the signals
in my frontal lobe that produce a motor-coordinated response
without my conscious awareness of it, you know?
      Instinct.
      Reflex.
It's natural, natural; it's a natural process that changes the dimensions
of my face, altering my whole bearing because people, I imagine,
when they look upon this visage, this frontage, what they're thinking is:
      What a lot of gravity –
      there it is, gravity manifest,
      the downward drag
      of the material world
      held in a single human profile,
but, you see, that's just my face, just the way it is –
      unreconstructed,
      unadulterated,
but what a thing to have to greet all living organisms with, you know?
And I do frequently wonder if the mind creates the face or the face
creates the mind and where even is the mind in relation to the face?
      Is the mind positioned
      behind the face?
      Is that
      where it lurks?

When I look in the mirror I sometimes think I can see my thoughts
rippling beneath the skin, sometimes almost protruding out of cracks
in my forehead, but most times there is no sense of proximity between
the two –

>	the fleshy thing there in the glass
>	and the thinking thing
>	narrating the fleshy thing's presence
>	are nowhere near each other;

and what the thinking thing seems to be is a reoccurrence of an anonymous voice

>	housed in a secret location
>	sent to spy on the fleshy thing.

And, you know, it was that dislocation I remember during our training
session last week. As we were sitting in our communication circle
on the fifth floor, tables pushed to the walls, I couldn't be sure what,

>	if anything,
>
>	was *me*.

So when Paula asked everyone to begin by saying our favourite word,
these two remote things – the fleshy and the thinking – separately
observed our colleagues utter words such as

>	*glimmer*
>	*orchid*
>	*auspicious*
>	*drainage*

supragenic

now

and you, Rob, you saying *fedora*, each syllable springing from your tongue, lips, and teeth so gleefully –

fe

do

ra

It's fun and mysterious, you said, and everyone agreed when Paula said a word had never so perfectly represented the spirit of its speaker, so absolutely

captured

the sense of playful mischief that you bring to the world of Quality Assurance, so you did, as Paula said, absolutely smash that exercise, and then, of course, I had to go next. There were murmurs of *tough act to follow* and from afar the thinking thing smirked as it watched the fleshy thing squirm and stutter, unsure of how it usually produced coherent sounds, it was floundering and I think

me,

the I –

a third thing to contend with –

was flitting between the other two things, split in my allegiances as the thinking thing was justified in its contempt of that gormless lump of skin but then that wretched fleshy thing was so abandoned, so vulnerable and alone, and what could it do? What options, really, did it have? So, in the end, the word was just ejaculated with no aplomb, just spat into existence as a statement of some kind of personal truth:

contain

contain

because I like con- words,
am satisfied by
a thing within a thing
and I'll tell you what, I saw Paula's grimace that she tried to hide with a clap,
a thoroughly condescending gesture of applause for the *very interesting choice,*
Sophie. I know what that meant. I got the acknowledgment of my dullness,
my dourness, my drippiness; I know that's what *contain* signalled to everyone
and at that moment I accepted it; I accepted that no one could ever know of my
schisms, that the fleshy thing was a lone actor, with thinking a distinct entity laughing
away whilst somewhere else entirely. But later on, after I'd sat on the train next to
a woman with endocrinological heat-patches
crawling down her cleavage
as I thought about dinner, and then got home and made and ate dinner, and
washed-up and sat on a kitchen chair for a bit, and then undressed and took
my make-up off and brushed my teeth and got into bed and scrolled through
my phone for an hour, and then turned off the light and made shapes in the darkness,
then I realised:

No.
Contain isn't my favourite word.
It repulses me,
horrifies me.
I am disgusted
by its borders,
its withinness.

The fleshy thing does not and cannot speak for all the multitudes of Sophie.
To speak for all that is not possible. A person is absolutely ineffable, aren't they?
So, if I could go back in time to that moment, first of all I'd say *The thing is, Paula,*

> *you cannot expect*
> *to learn anything*
> *from anyone*
> *with one word*

and then, secondly, I'd look her straight in the eyes and say *But if you do insist on playing this game, then the word I'm going to choose is*

> *circumvent*
> *because I like*
> *getting around*
> *all the many things*
> *that come to block*
> *the way*

and I enjoy imagining the ridges appearing between Paula's brows as she struggles to comprehend the shock of this word, the impact of its plurality on her singular self – the singular unit of Paula unable to break free of itself, hemmed in by its own limits, its ordinary oneness forming a predictably meshed thinking and fleshy thing that's all ego as, y'know Paula, she's such a manager, a narrativiser, a talker, a player, a real pro. Don't you agree, Rob?

...

Uh-huh

...

Uh-huh

...

Yeah, yeah

...

Mmm, well...

...

Really?

...

But tell me Rob,
why do you think that?"

WORK OUT

below John's septum the slanted strip of his philtrum draws Jane
to it with its insouciance   its lazy gait   as his upper lip engages
in a performance of itself prior to passing thirty-eight years of age
this strip of skin can preoccupy Jane sometimes
like drinking enough water
like earwax draining videos
like shipping cancelled celebrity pairings

and more than the man around it this strip of skin gives the impression
of being an entity   an ordinance that shrugs off the form of its hours
contained in designated spaces   a participant in laborious conversations
carried out to service ends neither Jane nor John can see for themselves

and Jane now notices the disappearing liquid in their glasses and it's
obvious they must be refilled if they're to continue being accomplices
in the retrieval of each other's feelings about their experiences

because every person deserves to be purged   thinks Jane
while considering
if John believes the same
if his thoughts mirror hers
if the scenarios she pictures
are ones he also pictures

meaning that when they are both at their desks during the day
doing separate tasks   their backs facing
and their gazes directed towards unrelated objects
the hidden contents of their minds are united
in imagining the emptying out of their respective souls
so each becomes visible
and washed away

that is

Jane's soul
is seen and removed
John's soul
is seen and removed

Jane and John's
inner presences
appear and disappear

John and Jane's
souls become
gone together

and with their glasses full again Jane realises
she can now only see John's face in pieces   his left eye   his right cheek

his jaw   his forehead
there is no whole
cohesion cannot be found

and she stops him to agree   to say   yes yes
she recognises too
that the morality issue of our age
is the dominance of first-person prose

and Jane keeps saying
yes yes yes
to make sure John knows
she knows
how he feels

as it's incredibly important that
he knows she knows
he must if nothing else
know right now that
she knows him
she gets him
others don't
get him or know him
they skirt around him
terrified of the truth

but

Jane and John

John and Jane

she must know
he knows
she knows

if she doesn't know   she thinks
all will be lost
they will be lost
they will lose themselves

to the chaos
of their own voices

but Jane doesn't know
how she can know
that he knows
she knows

and as John drinks and speaks
Jane drinks and thinks

but has she ever known
that someone has known
she's known

is it possible to really know
that someone knows
she knows

or is it that when conversation
has faded away
neither Jane nor John will know
what the other one knows
or doesn't know

is that the way it must be

but what if she wills it
what if she wills it with all her strength

she will will it
she will will
that he knows
she needs to know
that he knows
she knows

she will will
she will

WORK ON

Oh yes

Works of art hang
From the walls
Of the right minds

The wrong minds
Are empty

Corridors

Continuing

Failing

To end themselves

i watch her turn up to me daily
and get hard and complicate
the subjugation

the subjugation of voices
telling me

to stop
seeing her this way

i picture her disgraced
and come

and what if remembering is screaming?

what if vile bags of words move through my veins instead of blood?

what then?

WORK UP

WHEN IS IS WHEN THE CEILING STARTS FOLDING IN
WHEN CHAIRS DISAPPEAR THE FLOOR HAS A DIFFERENT FEEL
IS WHEN IT'S OVER WHEN IT'S TIME TO GO
GO HOME GO TO SLEEP
GET UP GO TO WORK
WORK ALL DAY
ALL DAYS REPEATING
ALL DAYS AN IMITATION IMITATING MYSELF EVERY DAY
FACILITATING MACHINES MAKING MACHINES
IMITATE HUMANS
AND HUMANS IMITATE MACHINES
GOT TO KEEP ON KEEP IT TOGETHER DO NOT BREAK
TOLERATE THE MACHINES TOLERATE THE HUMANS
ENDURE ENDURE ENDURE
ENDURE SOPHIE
WHAT IS CALLED LIFE MAY WELL BE DEATH IN THE END
BUT DON'T LOOK AT PAULA DON'T LET ON TO HER
NO
DON'T

FUCK
JUST DON'T
JUST GET BACK OUT THERE LIKE A MACHINE
ONE MORE HAVE ONE MORE
TALK TO JOHN ASK ABOUT HIS HOUSE HIS
HIEROGLYPHS COURSE
ASK ABOUT HIS WIFE AND HIS BABY
ASK HOW HE'S FINDING FATHERHOOD DOES HE FEEL FULFILLED
DOES HE RECOMMEND IT
DOES HE LOOK AT HIS DAUGHTER AND KNOW HIS PURPOSE
IGNORE YOUR GUT
IGNORE IGNORE IGNORE
ROB BE A MACHINE WITH SPIRIT
WHERE IS IT WHERE'S THAT SPIRIT THAT PHANTOM THAT
SPECTRE
WHERE'S IT LURKING
IS IT IN MY SKULL WHERE I DON'T FEEL IT
FEEL NOTHING NOTHING BUT SICKNESS
GOTTA CONJURE IT SUMMON IT
FIND THAT SPIRIT
THEN I'LL TALK TO PAULA THEN I'LL TELL HER

EVERY DAY AN ACHIEVEMENT
EVERY DAY A MIRACLE
ISN'T IT
ISN'T IT
IT IS NOT
IT IS
IT IS
IS IT
ISN'T IT JUST

WORK THROUGH

I'm often told I don't sound like I'm from
        where I'm from
So I feel like I'm from nowhere

People preparing to regret step onto the
        night bus
still drenched in the night out
drips of the sesh pooling on the floor
its wetness being tread up to the top deck
where streaks of latent bondage stain
        the aisle

I'd never have said you're even English

Oh but how are we to know our true origins?

The woman speaking is a premonition
She's 15 years to the future of me
She has the lived-in-ness that comes for us all

skin
bones
organs
blood
nerves

Do I live in them
or they live in me?

I start scrolling

But this woman is persistent
Persisting through my resistance to her
She talks about her marriage
She describes her dogs' exact colourings
She dissects her most egregious compromises
She complains about her manager
He isn't half full of himself
for such an unremarkable man

I see a succession of images of people I know

        and people I don't know
It makes me seasick
The difference between the two gets harder to discern

Is it possible to hallucinate intimacy with such fervour
that this psychic energy becomes its own kind of intimate act?

There's just so many unremarkable people, aren't there?

Four men in their mid-to-late twenties splay
        themselves on the seats in front of us

The entitlement of their vowels tickling the
        backs of their throats
as they spit sound into fluorescent light
        showing up the blood shot
through eyes searching for signs of recognition
        both obvious and not

I say to the woman that I have to encourage my team
        members to fully embody their talent
What does that mean?
I don't know
In team meetings I claim things like
It's important to be clear on your KPIs
And this is supposed to motivate them

But given that a person is brought into life
Is a riddle of cosmic dust
Is a never-was never-will-be-again
Is beset with urge and restraint
Is barely a moment
Is the end of the means
It is a lot to burden them with the prospect
        of doubt over indicators of their worth

So do you like your job, Paula?

One of the men eats parma ham straight from
        a plastic packet
Holding the meat between his forefinger and thumb
        he dangles it from a height over his mouth

I watched Rob perform a similar act with some processed
        turkey slices a few weeks ago
His lower jaw swinging wide open
It struck me that we cannot extricate ourselves
        from mechanisms

We depend on hinges to reveal holes
so things can go in and out

It's crucial that there's demarcated
        inside space and outside space
Vital for a sense of *this* and *that*

But as a 15 year-old virgin something seemed off
        to me about being
        designated inside space

I was far too 2-D for that

Could not really cope with any sorts of
        comings and goings
Wanted no entries and no exits

The cheer from downstairs is giving
        ritualistic
This is a journey between states after all
From the ecstatic to the dubious

Limbs wave
Heads undulate
as reggaeton plays on a speaker

The descent from upper to lower
        is an overturned caterpillar
a wailing creature on the verge of metamorphosis

The driver issues a warning about standing
        on the stairs

I watch Sophie's story
Lucky to work with such amazing people
        is written over the team picture

Three weeks ago I told her her KPIs were low
I said it indicated a lack of focus
That she was distracted from her task
        of reviewing content
That content is constantly churning more content
That it cannot be stopped
That it is produced and seen and produced
        ad infinitum
That content comes from us
        and we then come out of content
That without content there is no way to know
        if we are still breathing or not breathing
The thing about content review, I said, *is that*
after a while you can become a content specialist
You can specialise in content
And it's part of my job to help you get to that level
But you must commit yourself fully to reviewing
        the content first
You must subject yourself to all its possibilities
You must be content with the unstoppable utopia
        of content that comes your way

As I spoke, I smiled at her reassuringly
I wanted her to believe that I believed she believed
        in the workings of this system

Because if neither of us believed in it
we'd surely be in for an almighty reckoning
        one of these days

The woman behind me is voice noting a friend
She describes an incident between a couple
        they know
All through the night there were little hints
        these niggles and digs
going back and forth and back and forth
like two people who'd forgotten they usually
        make the effort to tolerate each other
Then it all came out

I did think, though, that she was going to batter him

A certain kind of glee
a certain kind of knowing
in her unfolding
of their scenario

Thing is, now all their savings have been lost to his figurine habit, innit?

The woman next to me asks if I live with
        someone special
I say I have two flatmates who I trust with my life
but who may or may not know my last name

Would you ever think of getting your own place?

After rent, bills, and debts the amount of money
        I have left is enough to briefly forget
that I do not really have any money to speak of

One of my flatmates saw John leave my room at 3 am
She would've heard the noises through the wall
        lifted from the performances
of people making a living on a planet inhabited
        by a species
driven to watch productions of itself reproducing

The week after I couldn't get into the bathroom
        as this flatmate was bent over the toilet
        unable to overcome her body
Her voice through the door was the texture of a
        cloud stuck to the ceiling

It quivered through its delicacy
Disavowed the act of poisoning oneself for fun
Promised it would all be over soon

I often think of how the phrase *I know how you live*
      is meant to be so damning

The man with the Parma ham has some arms on him
And I would have them surround me
I would feel them like bars across my chest
        while he entered me

I wish my desire were less manipulated

When John fucks me I think of the
        hunger for god
I mean the possibility of being known
        by the unknowable
I mean let me be had
Let me get gotten
and be getting got as flavoured
        mists shade skin pressing
        in on more skin pressing in

I mean can I manipulate want to not want
        what's wanting inside of me?

I push through a group of teenagers
        grinding surfaces against surfaces

Two girls kissing right in front of the back doors
so I dip under the arch of saliva between their
        parting lips

Street lamps partition my road
Each placed in the gap between the outer walls
       of every other house
Isosceles triangles created in the points of
       outer wall
       lamp
       outer wall

I don't believe in numbers

I know of one, two, three, four, and so on
But surely it's just a coping mechanism
A human delusion to make sense of a world
       we can perceive but never know
Symbols of a desperation to quantify the infinite

I do believe in shapes

I taste circles
I swallow oblongs
I itch triangles wriggling down
       my spine

And when I close my eyes I see
       all the polygons

roaming the plains
redrawing the land

to surround all those who live on it

and now I'm aware I'm drunk and swerving slightly but managing always managing to
make it somewhere to be in for 8:30 tomorrow
and dance on Saturday have a few lines a few dabs drink continuously from
9 pm to 11 am and sleep all Sunday to get through the week that comes after
to go drinking again on a Thursday and be gifted with the absence in the night the
stillness
that seems crafted as on a film set where every object and entity have
been selected and arranged like even the fox running from
pavement to pavement
is directed by a handler to be captured by my pov as I look out from this world at
that world and I am sick of these boundaries I don't want to be in or out I want
to go through I mean traverse states like when I told Rob I didn't think it was a good
idea and his eyes went down he retreated turned away and now decades may pass on
the fly without word because it's in or out no through just in or out
stuck in this or that state and but the thing with John is that no one can know and it's
no good no use really but it is so so good and there are sensations that remove the past
from the present because he does not inhibit he releases and yes it can't last and it's
fine it's fine it's all fine I'm a slip-in woman aren't I I am but a fake gun do be a real
gun all the same sometimes and if I ask did I do I can answer I did do at least this one
time I did do and here in front of the safety gates of my flat there's uncle socks hanging
on the washing line
uncle writing it's a fine thing to be making
your way in the city in my birthday card in the package of socks and bottle of zinc
& vits d, c & e a real lung fixer a tummy tucker vital in the bull rush of it all
and there's that fox again car loitering

all directed for my observation this car licking creature savouring
a splatter of materials to keep up its sustenance
before it's back to the breeding tank
and it looks up to see me staring and it stares back
terror taking over
it runs beneath a nest
of white tables and disappears all for me to see myself
reflected in its instinct
to make a point about these
cranium sinisters conspiring
and the belly mind rumbling
fearing
all the outside that's gotten on the inside
all the inside that's bleeding out

My window is a rain drum

    Undertaker blue
    underneath my eyes

A scene from the TV programme about teachers
    Sinéad mentioned
    comes to me just before sleep:

    a woman walking down a corrridor
    a man watching her walk away
    their colleagues watching him watch her

LIFE

PLASTICS

Every day an app asks me
how I'm feeling
Today I was tapping that
I have no symptoms

when there was a push notification
to say that we may all be
infertile by 2045

I was alone in my rented room

And I wasn't planning on reproducing anyway

I think I felt sorta resigned
about the whole thing
the childlessness –
en masse and personal

I dunno

I can only think I feel

IN THE YEARS WHEN NO VESSELS WERE FLIGHTS

Today I woke up at 6:32 am to see the sun rise
like a terrifying godhead shedding
its angry red skin onto the trembling skyline

I can be found in bed until midday more days than not
Though it's said I have a decent job

I was ordered to accept the things
I cannot change from an early age

Digging ever deeper down only dampens
the dirt already dragged over the decking anyway

I suppose I want everything
I don't know I need

I want it now

PLAGUE TIMES

I was 28 searching Père Lachaise
for Proust's tombstone, wandering
through the trees and graves as the air of spirits
licked my neck in the woods, probably thinking
how the year before I was struck
by the terror of ageing
in *Time Regained*:
it must be, I'd thought,
that *we* stop before we get old,
and then, after,
what continues
is a grotesque appropriation of our flesh.
Later, when I was drunk on free wine from a bookshop,
I tried to describe the grave to an American
but all I had was the capitalised surname
and a youthful love of emptiness.

Now at 36, in plague times, I find myself alone
and I find myself in a multi-season show
with many incomplete arcs for many forgotten guest stars.
And 36 is not old but it's old enough
to see life being done to me and
to come across posts by actors from 90s' cult TV

whose characters
used to occupy my mind
in that total way only unreal people can,
with their imagined worlds burrowing
into the roots of my futures,
a wholeness of hypotheticals
and non-corporeal communities;
and now the faces I see on a smaller screen

aren't the ones I grew up with:
they are dodgy masks worn by strangers
yet they are cruel revelations
as they are a forced participation in years.
I do not recognise them as I do not recognise myself
in their transformations.

When Cassandra spoke of the coming devastation
she was told her prophesies were preposterous.

Cassandra's life is one of normal things:
she sits around or goes for long walks;
she speaks to loved ones over screens;
she distracts herself with cultural ephemera
or lets her feelings seep into the furniture

so she can observe them as objects
to eventually be discarded.

I went out to the pier and watched the sea
be interrupted by an island

It's strange how I have this continuity within me
when so many selves have perished

The unstoppable regularity of the tide terrifies me
There are some days when you know the world is ancient
and you know your place in it is temporary
and you realise you have to live with knowing
all is out there and real
yet still a figment
of the waters swelling inside of you

and, I'm finding, ageing starts to become a plea –

please, please, please
let me mean something
and let me mean nothing at all

A PERSON OF

By 18 January 2021 there've been 942 US homicides so far
On the same website the global number of
Births per second continually mounts
There's exact amounts of living and dying in me
I think
Some breathable eras too
But I don't know about longevity
Ask anyone who's ever met me and they'll say not a thing
About a person of no colour
A person drained
I wonder if all people wish to separate their outline from their substance
In the centre of town there was once a brick with my name on it
There amongst all the other bricks in the hospital building
And it remained for several months as a possible fever dream
As it was never commented on by anyone
And when I saw it I was unsure if the name was ever mine
I thought there's someone else who's been called forth
From these letters that walks around with fuller feelings and firmer meaning
If I've changed it's that I now regard the word *Bildungsroman* with suspicion
But of course if the world really starts to crumble where will I begin
Murderers sometimes share cells with thieves
I woke up with loose associations amongst seen and unseen entities
And the image of a collection of nouns that read

Gut inscrutability brush line mongoose decade
It's the 340th day of survival
And there is love and longing
The death rate per second is about half the birth rate still
So all you see on the counter is addition
This is the last time I refuse my eyelids their closure
I swear
But aren't we in need of help and excavation
An uprooting

SAINT MARGERY WITHOUT

such is devotion
such is longing
that I've forgotten how to swallow
I've deactivated my masseter
first comes dryness
the discomfort of
discarded organs
ceasing
then starvation:
validation
       – a feeling of
         abundance
         via lack

And
my god
I'd really love to hate you
but all my suffering
has just got to
get done

WINDOWS MIGHT

we are walled in at the end of someone else's corridor
and you talk about the death of a man you loved
while our room suffers no disturbances of itself
but this man has been on your mind
like   you say his soles have been pressing
on the surface of thought

he is not my father

and   you say the problem with that kind of love –
the one between you and this other man –
is that it treads all over the senses until
seeing doesn't really feel like seeing anymore

we can't know from where we are within these walls
if anyone might refer to now as day or night
and the mono-ness of the room hushes us
which leads me to wonder –
when will i next savour the weight of someone else's body
and what will it be like for me when you're gone

like is it possible that my life without you will ever replace my life with you

can you imagine absolute nothingness   i ask
no no   you say but perhaps nothingness imagines us
maybe death is a nothingness that invokes all our disappearances

i have this persistent feeling that my sight is darkening
that i am the night
that it is not the result of orbits
but a well filling up from the bottom of my stomach
the fluid rising
spilling out of my open mouth and into the world
around me

this room has no sense of pity for us   i say
it doesn't   you agree   and our eyes can't offer any alternatives
as we only see the limits of what we're given
something every prison cell   every gaoler   relies on
so we won't ourselves   with our own eyes
be able to bring down the walls' regime
but windows might

ACKNOWLEDGEMENTS

Thanks are due to the editors of the following publications, in which a number of these poems have appeared: *PDF*, *Spectra Poets*, *SINK! Magazine*, *Drunk Monkeys*, and *Compass Rose Literary Journal*.

A huge thanks to Randolph Healy, whose enthusiasm and support has made this project possible.

Thanks to the Arts Council of Ireland for the Agility Award in 2024, which has enabled me to have time to focus on writing. I have also been in the control group for the 'Basic Income for Artists' pilot research scheme. I am incredibly grateful for the research they are doing and what it has given to artists in Ireland. I hope it can continue.

And all my love and thanks to my friends and family, who I feel incredibly lucky to have. Especially my mum. This is for her.

www.ingramcontent.com/pod-product-compliance
Lightning Source LLC
Chambersburg PA
CBHW051423070526
44584CB00023B/3557